CHRISTMAS TIME IS HERE

7 Arrangements for Brass Quintet

Selections from The Canadian Brass CD
(Opening Day Entertainment Group)

This Trumpet II part also includes one selection for Flugelhorn.

ISBN 978-1-4803-6035-8

THE CANADIAN

BRASS

DISTRIBUTED BY

HAL•LEONARD®
CORPORATION

7777 W. BLUEMOUND RD. P.O. BOX 13819 MILWAUKEE, WI 53213

www.canadianbrass.com
www.halleonard.com

CONTENTS

ANGEL CHOIR AND THE TRUMPETER

Music and Lyrics by Chris Dedrick
Adapted by Chris Coletti

Trumpet in B♭

BACH'S BELLS

Inspired by Bach's BWV 29 and
Leontovych's CAROL OF THE BELLS

Chris Coletti

HARK, THE HERALD ANGELS SING

Felix Mendelssohn
Arranged by Brandon Ridenour

Somewhat freely

Moderately - in tempo

Trumpet II in B♭

MY LITTLE DRUM

By Vince Guaraldi
Arranged and adapted by Brandon Ridenour

SKATING

Trumpet in B♭

By Vince Guaraldi
Arranged by Brandon Ridenour

(opt. all slurred)

Bright Jazz Waltz (♩ = 180–200)

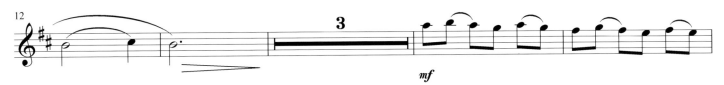

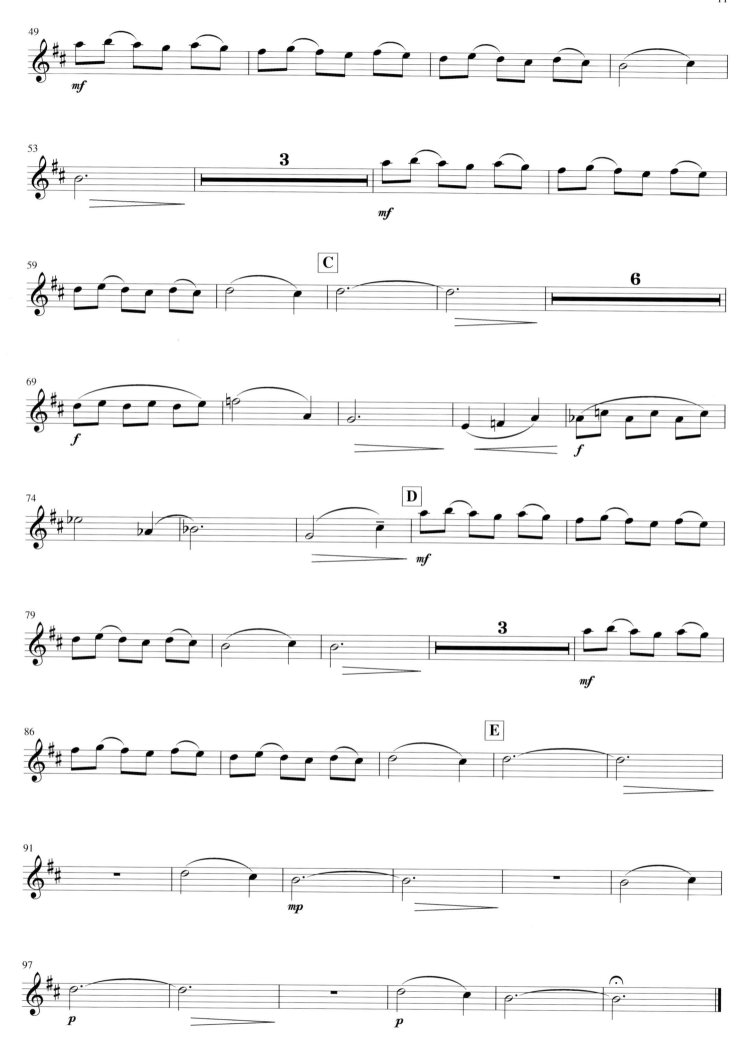

O TANNENBAUM

Traditional
Arranged by Vince Guaraldi
Adapted by Brandon Ridenour

WHAT CHILD IS THIS?

Traditional
Arranged and adapted by Brandon Ridenour

Jazz Waltz (♩ = 120–130)